GO FACTS **SPACE**
Teaching Guide

Contents

A & C BLACK • LONDON

Introducing Go Facts

The Reading and Writing Link

Each of the *Go Facts* books is a model of well-written, accurate and easy-to-read nonfiction. The writers have used selected nonfiction structures to help their readers better understand information, ideas and issues. When pupils are made aware of these structures, they are able to comprehend texts at a higher level. They experiment with the structures and conventions modelled by the writers, and so learn to use these structures in their own writing. The *Go Facts* series has been developed to foster this reading and writing link.

Writing in a Balanced Literacy Programme

Regular writing is as important as regular reading. During shared, guided and independent reading sessions, pupils read a range of texts, construct their meaning and learn comprehension strategies. In sahred, guided and independent writing sessions, pupils learn to think about, plan, draft, revise and share their work as writers. Just as with guided reading lessons, guided writing lessons allow the teacher to give explicit instruction in targeted skills and strategies.

The teaching plan in this guide is flexible, allowing numerous possibilities for practice of each step of the writing process. Throughout, there is strong support for teachers, including detailed notes showing how to model strategies in each step of the writing process.

Stages in the Writing Process

The writing process involves five stages:

1 **Prewriting and planning:** This is the preparation stage in which pupils choose the topic and determine the audience and purpose of the piece. They read, research, discuss and brainstorm the topic to gather thoughts and ideas. Then they write the main idea. They list keywords, take notes and cross out ideas not relevant to topic, audience and purpose.

2 **Drafting:** This is the organisation stage and first attempt at writing. Ideas that could go together are grouped in sentences and paragraphs, and the ideas numbered in the order in which they are to be written.

3 **Revising:** Pupils clarify and improve their work at whole piece, paragraph, sentence and word level. They check for topic sentences, clear ideas and supporting details, logical order and linking words. They read the piece aloud, or think about how it will sound to a partner.

4 **Editing:** This is the polishing stage at which style, grammar, spelling, punctuation and setting-out is checked.

5 **Publishing:** This is the stage at which the writing is made available to others. It is motivation for revising and editing. Not all writing needs to be published.

During the Writing Nonfiction lessons, pupils will not always take a piece of writing from stage one to stage five. They may work on portions of reports as they practise skills and strategies, rather than going through the whole process each time. A finished product is not always the goal. The goal is for pupils to learn and practise each step of writing an information report. Brainstorming, grouping facts and ideas, formulating topic sentences, creating graphics and captions: these are all important skills for writing nonfiction texts.

Using Go Facts: Space

The *Go Facts: Space books* link literacy with other areas of the curriculum. The books are ideal for use within or outside literacy lessons and can be used to link with QCA units such as: Science Unit 5E: Earth, Sun and Moon; Unit 6E Forces in Action.

The *Go Facts* pupil books are written at reading and interest levels appropriate for the upper primary years. It is suggested that they are used with more able pupils in Year 5 and average and able pupils in Year 6.

This *Teaching Guide* includes lesson notes on reading nonfiction and writing nonfiction for each title in *Go Facts: Space*. To teach the reading and writing of information (non-chronological) reports systematically, work through the order in which they are presented. These lessons will help pupils to progress towards achieving the Core Learning in Literacy Objectives (*Primary Framework for Literacy and Mathematics,* 2006) identified for each lesson.

Reading the Nonfiction Text

The reading lessons in this guide are suitable for small groups, and will fit easily into guided reading sessions. The lessons explicitly teach effective reading strategies for processing information reports. The teacher introduces the text and selects the teaching points, before pupils read the text independently. The lesson notes include discussion points to encourage oral responses from pupils. This provides an opportunity for further teaching. At the end of the lesson pupils can complete a written response on the worksheet.

Using the Writing Nonfiction Lesson Notes

By following up each reading lesson with a lesson in writing nonfiction, pupils learn to use the same structures and strategies modelled in the *Go Facts* books in their own nonfiction writing. If the writing lessons are taught in sequence, by the end of the series pupils will have worked on an information report through all the stages of the writing process.

During the lessons, the teacher sometimes models a writing strategy by thinking aloud while writing. Pupils might also participate by telling the teacher what to write, or by helping to plan and write some of the text.

The Writing Nonfiction lessons are suitable for small groups or the whole class. They encompass guided writing, independent writing and research. They could be used over a two-day period, by teaching the strategy on day one, and then having the pupils apply the strategy and share their work on day two.

Using the Writing Mini-lessons

Mini-lessons with worksheets cover each stage of the writing process. Although they sometimes refer specifically to one book, the ideas in these Mini-lessons can be used by teachers for other books in the *Go Facts* series, depending on the needs of the pupils and the stage of their writing. Some of the Mini-lesson worksheets can be reused with different content.

Assessment

Teachers can use the Assessment Checklist to record a pupil's progress in writing information reports by entering a date in the three columns. The worksheets provide opportunities for informal assessment throughout the reading and writing sessions.

Models for Nonfiction Writing

The books in *Go Facts: Space* make information accessible in content, layout, language and writing style. This allows readers to participate actively and to concentrate on the learning opportunities offered by the text. It also allows young readers to internalise the structures and conventions of nonfiction writing for their own use. The large photographs can be used to bring out readers' background knowledge and interests.

The nonfiction elements that are modelled in this *Go Facts* set include:

Information reports

Go Facts: Space focuses on reading and writing information reports. Each page begins with an opening statement.

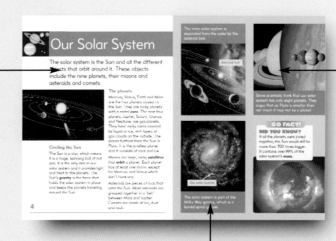

Photographs

Large exciting photographs draw readers into the text and get them thinking about the topic.

Captions and labels

Captions and labels support the written text or provide added details. They also invite the reader to move in many different directions to find information.

Text types

Explanations, instructions, recounts and discussions are all included in the *Go Facts: Space* set.

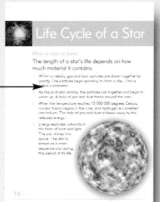

Visual literacy

Diagrams convey information clearly and memorably, and give the opportunity to teach important visual literacy skills. A range of photos, diagrams, cross-sections, tables, maps and timelines is introduced across the series.

Paragraphs

Information reports in *Go Facts: Space* are extended to include more complex paragraph structures, such as cause and effect, compare and contrast, problem and solution.

Elements of Nonfiction Writing

Go Facts: Space models the following text structures.

Information (Non-chronological) Reports

Purpose

The purpose of a report is to give facts and details about a topic, eg natural disasters. Reports focus on features and attributes common to all things within that group. Other forms of nonfiction writing are often embedded in information reports, such as *description, explanation, instructions, recount* and *discussion*. Reports differ from explanations in that they don't have to explain how or why.

Structure

1 General opening statement or description of a class of things
2 Series of paragraphs about the topic beginning with topic sentences followed by supporting statements and detailed evidence, often in the form of statistics
3 There is often no ending to an information report, but there can be a concluding statement, a warning or a call for action.

Language features

- language is usually unemotional, impersonal and formal, in the 3rd person
- the 'timeless' present tense is usually used and sometimes the passive
- specialised nouns, adjectives and verbs name and describe the topic
- connecting words tie the sentences and paragraphs tightly together

Paragraph Structures

Reports can be extended to include the following features:

Compare and Contrast

A comparison paragraph structure is used to compare objects, events or ideas.
- starts with a topic sentence
- shows similarities and differences between objects, events or ideas

Problem and Solution

A problem-and-solution structure is used to present a problem and its solution.
- starts with a statement outlining the problem
- suggests a solution to the problem

Cause and Effect

A cause-and-effect structure is used to describe why or how something happens.
It shows the relationship between two things and how one thing makes the other happen.
- states the cause
- states the effects, including secondary effects if any (the effects can be stated before the cause)

Visual Elements

Reports often contain visual elements such as diagrams, photos, maps, and timelines that carry extra information or support the written text.
There are also:

Sequence Flow Diagrams

Sequence Flow Diagrams show a sequence of steps. They are useful in summarising a process, or showing changes (including cause and effect) over time.
- a heading sets the context of the diagram
- words and arrows show the order in which events happen
- labels identify things (nouns) or processes (verbs)
- processes may be represented by arrows
- captions summarise or explain the diagram

Cross-sections

A cross-section reveals the inside or hidden parts of a subject. It shows in one plane how the parts are connected.
- shows the subject in one plane as if a layer has been cut away
- captions explain how the parts are connected
- labels name parts of the diagram

Go Facts: Space Overview

	Text and Paragraph Structures	Visual Literacy or Graphics	Other Features
GO FACTS SPACE The Universe	Explanation plus: Information Report pp. 4–5 Compare and Contrast p. 11 Cause and Effect pp. 16–19 Problem and Solution pp. 20, 23 Argument pp. 24–25	Objects in Space pp. 6–7 Colour Diagrams pp. 17, 19 Diagram Superimposed on Photos p. 26 Star Maps pp. 28–29 Fact Table p. 30 Colour Photos throughout – incl. long exposures from space Varied font size and colours	Table of Contents Index Glossary Fact Boxes Captions Cross-sections
GO FACTS SPACE Our Future in Space	Information Report plus: Problem and Solution pp. 4–5, 8–13, 18–19, 22–25 Factual Recount pp. 6–7, 16–17 Instructions pp. 14–15 Argument pp. 20–21 Conclusion pp. 26–29	Colour Photos throughout Table p. 30	Table of Contents Index Glossary Fact Boxes Captions Table
GO FACTS SPACE The Solar System	Information Report plus: Cause and Effect pp. 10–19, 22, 24–27 Factual Recount pp. 22–23 Problem and Solution (elements of) pp. 22–23 Instructions pp. 22–23	Model of the Solar System pp. 6–7 Diagram Phases of the Moon p. 27 Colour Photos throughout Table p. 30	Table of Contents Index Glossary Fact Boxes Captions
GO FACTS SPACE Exploring Space	Information Report plus: Factual Recount pp. 4–5, 11–13, 15, 18–21, 23 Explanation pp. 6–17, 21–27 Cause and Effect pp. 19, 21 Discussion p. 24 Instructions pp. 28–29 Timeline p. 30	Colour Photos throughout Photo of Painting p. 4 Cross-section p. 28 Timeline p. 30	Table of Contents Index Glossary Fact Boxes Captions

Reading Nonfiction	Writing Nonfiction	Writing Process Mini-lessons
TEACHING FOCUS Locating information to answer questions using a variety of methods **Y5 Strand 7** Make notes on and use evidence from across a text to explain events, ideas **Y6 Strand 7** Appraise a text quickly, deciding on its value, quality or usefulness	**Prewriting and Drafting:** Sketching, writing labels, and captions for nonfiction **Y5 Strand 9** Adapt non-narrative forms and styles to write fiction or factual texts, including poems **Y6 Strand 10** Use varied structures to shape and organise text coherently **Prewriting and Drafting:** Explanatory writing **Y5 Strand 10** Experiment with the order of sections and paragraphs to achieve different effects **Y6 Strand 10** Use varied structures to shape and organise text coherently	**Prewriting:** Getting information by asking and answering questions **Prewriting and Drafting:** Organising information
TEACHING FOCUS Organising categories and keywords into paragraphs **Y5 Strand 7** Distinguish between everyday use of words and their subject-specific use **Y6 Strand 7** Explore how word meanings change when used in different contexts	**Drafting and Writing:** Problem and solution paragraphs **Y5 Strand 11** Adapt sentence construction to different text types, purpose and readers **Y6 Strand 11** Express subtle distinctions of meaning by constructing sentences in varied ways **Drafting:** Understanding and using the passive **Y5 Strand 9** Adapt non-narrative forms and styles to write factual texts **Y6 Strand 9** Select words and languages drawing on their knowledge of formal writing	**Planning and Drafting:** Turning category headings and keywords into paragraphs Learning and reinforcing facts:
TEACHING FOCUS Learning and reinforcing information **Y5 Strand 7** Make notes on and use evidence from across a text to explain events, ideas **Y6 Strand 7** Understand underlying themes, causes and points of view	**Drafting and Writing:** Compare and contrast paragraphs **Y5 Strand 9** Adapt non-narrative forms and styles to write fiction and factual texts, including poems **Y6 Strand 10** Set their own challenges to extend achievement and experience in writing **Writing:** Writing comparisons **Y5 Strand 11** Adapt sentence construction to different text types, purposes and readers **Y6 Strand 11** Express subtle distinction of meaning by constructing sentences in varied ways	**Writing:** Compare and contrast paragraphs **Editing and Publishing:** Editing an information report
TEACHING FOCUS Visual literacy in information reports **Y5 Strand 7** Compare different types of information texts and identify how they are structured **Y6 Strand 7** Understand how writers use different structures to create coherence and impact	**Writing and Editing:** Cause and effect **Y5 Strand 10** Change the order of material within a paragraph, moving the topic sentence **Y6 Strand 10** Use paragraphs to achieve emphasis **Writing and Editing:** Editing paragraphs using sentence strips **Y5 Strand 9** Reflect independently and critically on their own writing and edit and improve it **Y6 Strand 6** Use a range of appropriate strategies to edit, proofread and correct spelling in their own work, on paper or on screen	

The Universe Reading Nonfiction

Teaching Focus
Locating information to answer questions

Y5 Strand 7 Make notes on and use evidence from across a text to explain events, ideas
Y6 Strand 7 Appraise a text quickly, deciding on its value, quality or usefulness

Lesson 1 preparation:
- copies of text *Go Facts: The Universe*
- copy of **WORKSHEET 1** for each pupil

Introducing the topic – The Universe
- Ask pupils to flip through *The Universe* and describe the way it is organised, eg cover, Contents page, text, graphics, Glossary and Index.
- Ask what they think of its layout, eg headings, paragraphing, fonts, bold type, bullets, italics, numbering and graphics.
- Ask pupils to look at each chapter title and ask one question they hope that chapter will answer.

Guided questions and discussion
The labels **'here, hidden, head and heart'** are used instead of '*literal, inferential, evaluative and response*', to describe different kinds of questions.
This kind of questioning helps assess the extent to which a pupil has understood the text, and also teaches comprehension.

Here **questions and answers (literal):**

The answers can be found 'here' in the text, usually in one sentence. We can point to the answer.
Why do astronomers keep measuring the Universe (p. 4)
How does dust and gas travel through space? (p. 4)
What is necessary for stars to form? (p. 4)
How is distance measured in the Universe? (p. 5)
How are stars classified? (p. 14)
Why does a star begin dying? (p. 18)
What is nuclear fusion? (Glossary)

Hidden **questions and answers (literal and inferential):**

The answers are usually in two or more places, including graphics. We may need to reorganise or summarise the information to make it relevant.
Why can't new stars form in elliptical galaxies? (pp. 4 and 10)
What holds stars and clusters together in galaxies? (p. 8)
What is one reason for the irregular shape of irregular galaxies? (p. 11)
Do stars stay the same throughout their life? (p. 14)
What does the colour of a star tell you? (pp. 14–15)
Why do stars shine? Do they really twinkle? (p. 15)
We cannot see black holes, so how do we know they are there? (p. 20)
If you wanted to find planets the size of Earth that are orbiting stars, how might you do so?

Head **questions and answers (literal and inferential and critical thinking):**

We use information from the text and graphics plus our imagination, experiences and background knowledge. We

judge and evaluate by asking if it is true, accurate, probable, desirable, acceptable. We make intelligent guesses to fill in gaps, or work things out by ourselves.
Why do we use light years rather than kilometres or miles to express distances in the Universe? (p. 5)
What is a black hole and what causes it? Do all stars end their lives in a super nova explosion? (pp. 20–21)
If you observed the sky at different times each night and at different seasons, would you find the constellations in the same part of the sky all the time? Explain. (p. 26)
The Earth doesn't really stand still, and the Sun doesn't really rise and set. Why did early astronomers think they did?

Heart **questions and answers (literal and inferential and critical thinking and response):**

Require emotional responses to the content, people, happenings, language and images.
What do you think about the Big Bang, Big Crunch and Big Freeze theories? (pp. 5, 24, 25 etc.)

Independent work on text comprehension
- Ask pupils to find items in the text that can be sequenced in order of size, intensity or distance, eg cold-cool-warm-hot.
- Pupils complete **Item 1** of **WORKSHEET 1**.

> **Answers:** (a) *star ′ constellation ′ galaxy ′ cluster ′ supercluster ′ Earth ′ Solar System ′ Milky Way Galaxy ′ The Universe;* (b) *blue-white ′ yellow ′ red*

- In pairs or groups, orally, pupils find a word from the text for which they'd like a definition, or a definition for which they'd like the word. Other pupils find the answers. (Use Glossary and Index.)
- Pupils complete **Item 2** of **WORKSHEET 1**.
- Ask pupils to suggest categories for a table to record information about the different types of galaxy. Pupils fill in information on the board.
- Pupils complete **Item 3** of **WORKSHEET 1**.

Summary of text types in *The Universe*
Cover Blurb – draws audience in, outlines main content.
The main text type is **Explanation.** Other features are:
pp. 4–5   Information Report
p. 11   Compare and Contrast elements.
pp. 16–19   Cause and Effect elements.
p. 20   Problem and Solution paragraph.
p. 23   Problem and Solution paragraph.
pp. 24–25   Exposition (argument).

Reading	Name
	Date

MAKING SENSE OF INFORMATION

1 Rewrite the following in order of the

a) smallest to largest:

constellation   supercluster   galaxy   cluster   star

_____

The Milky Way Galaxy   Earth   The Solar System   The Universe

_____

b) hottest to coolest:

yellow star   blue-white star   red star

_____

2 Draw lines to connect the words on the left with their meanings on the right:

stars	central part; place where new stars are formed
intergalactic	clouds of gas and dust
The Big Bang Theory	between galaxies
galaxies	spinning balls of hot gas that give off light
nucleus	belief that the Universe will eventually begin shrinking
halo	large system of stars drawn together by gravity
stellar	circle of light surrounding an object
nebulae	the belief that a giant explosion caused the Universe to expand
The Big Crunch	the distance that light travels in a year
a light year	to do with stars; relating to stars

3 Complete the following chart using information on pp. 10–11 of _The Universe._

TYPE OF GALAXY	SHAPE, SIZE and APPEARANCE	DO THEY CONTAIN NEW STARS? EXPLAIN WHY/NOT AND WHERE	HOW COMMON ARE THEY?	WHAT HAPPENS AT THEIR CENTRES?
Elliptical Galaxy				
Spiral Galaxy				
Barred-Spiral Galaxy				
Irregular Galaxy				

The Universe Writing Nonfiction

Teaching Focus
Drawings for information reports

Writing Process
Prewriting and drafting

Y5 Strand 9 Adapt non-narrative forms and styles to write fiction or factual texts, including poems
Y6 Strand 10 Use varied structures to shape and organise text coherently

Lesson 2 preparation:
- copies of *Go Facts: The Universe*
- copy of **WORKSHEET 2** for each pupil
- board/chart

Introducing the lesson
- In groups, pupils read pp. 8–13 of *The Universe* using the following method: going clockwise, the first pupil reads a paragraph aloud; the next asks a question about it; the next answers it; the next says what kind of question it is – here, hidden, head, heart (see Lesson 1).

Modelling the drawing strategy
- All pupils draw (in pencil) diagrams that sum up or clarify what they have just read.
- Pupils show their drawings to other pupils who guess and discuss what the drawing is about and suggest how the drawing could be improved.
- Pupils amend their drawings, and add labels, captions and arrows if necessary.
- Ask pupils what techniques they used in their drawings that helped improve them: eg how can you show which part of an object is brighter, or more important, or further away? How can you show that something is fuzzy, or well-defined?
- Record these tips on the board.
- Give each pupil a copy of **WORKSHEET 2** and read and discuss the drawing tips given on the bookmark. Add to it any other tips which the pupils suggested earlier.
- Pupils can later paste this bookmark on cardboard and cut out for future use.

Independent Practice
- Each pupil chooses one of the photos of a galaxy from *The Universe,* and describes orally, in detail, to a partner or group, what they see. The other pupils look at the photo during the description, and add to or amend the description when the pupil has finished describing it.
- **On WORKSHEET 2,** each pupil sketches the photo which they have just described, and writes a short caption to go with it. If further clarification is necessary, they should add short labels with arrows. Discuss how words such as 'the' can often be omitted in labels.

Homework
- Pupils pretend they are astronomers before the invention of the telescope, with only their naked eyes for observation. They look at the sky on a clear night, choose any astronomical feature that interests them, and draw it. They should note the date and time, and the position of the object in relation to other objects in the sky.
- Follow-up at school – pupils try to identify the drawn objects, and discuss the drawings. The **star maps** on pp. 28–29 of *The Universe* will help their orientation. Remind pupils which hemisphere they are observing the stars from.
- Based on this feedback, pupils amend their drawings, write captions and labels and add arrows and colours to their sketches if necessary.

Prewriting and Drafting

Name

Date

DRAWING HEAVENLY BODIES

Time of observation: _____

MATERIALS
- plain white paper.
- hard pencil (2H or 3) for well-defined objects.
- softer pencil (1 or 2) for fuzzy areas like clouds.
- an eraser to fix mistakes.

DRAWING TIPS FOR SCIENCE
- The **aim** of scientific drawings is to make the sketch look as much like the real object as possible.
- Choose a clear night and **OBSERVE** carefully. Notice the *shape* of what you want to draw, and its size and position in relation to surrounding objects.
- Draw the general outline.
- Look at the object again, searching for more details.
- Draw the details, beginning with the biggest and clearest ones.
- If you are drawing the stars around the main object, begin with the brightest one. Barely touch the page with your pencil to draw the faintest ones.
- For a fuzzy or cloudy effect, smudge the lines lightly with your finger.
- Keep comparing your drawing to the object you are drawing, and erase and redraw to fix mistakes. Drawing makes you notice more.
- Use labels, captions and arrows to make your sketch easier to understand.
- Arrows can show movement or parts of a process.

A & C Black

The Universe Writing Nonfiction

Teaching Focus
Explanatory writing

Writing Process
Prewriting and drafting

Y5 Strand 10 Experiment with the order of sections and paragraphs to achieve different effects
Y6 Strand 10 Use varied structures to shape and organise text coherently

Lesson 3 preparation:
- copies of text *Go Facts: The Universe*
- copy of **WORKSHEET 3** for each pupil
- sheet of A4 paper for each pupil and glue and scissors
- copy **WORKSHEET 3** onto an OHP transparency
- board/chart/overhead projector and markers

Introducing the lesson
- Explain that usually non-fiction books are information (non-chronological) reports that classify and describe topics with examples and details. However, they often have other text types within the report e.g. recounts, discussion, explanation.
- First, ask pupils to scan the text of *The Universe* to find examples of the structure of an explanation text: a title containing the words *How, Why* or *What*; a general introductory statement; a series of stages explaining how or why something happens.
- Next, pupils should find examples in the text of the language features of explanations, e.g. simple present tense, passive voice, formal and impersonal (third person), specialised vocabulary, cause and effect connectives (e.g. *because, as a result*), time connectives (e.g. *next, after, as, when, at this stage, when*).
- Tell pupils they are going to read about stars, and prepare an explanation on their life cycle. As they read the text, they should particularly notice the following stages that a star goes through in its life:

protostar → main sequence star → red giant → white dwarf → black dwarf (write these on the board).

- Pupils read pp. 14–18 of *The Universe* using the following method: going clockwise, the first pupil reads a paragraph aloud; the next asks a question about it; the next answers it.

Modelling
- Working from an OHP transparency of **WORKSHEET 3**, invite pupils to underline the verbs in the text. Discuss their tense (all present tense). Note the **passive** sentences in which the object comes first in the sentence, not the subject. This draws more attention to it, eg: **Gas and dust particles** in a nebula <u>are drawn</u> together by gravity. **This halo** <u>gets blown</u> away by released energy. **The star** <u>is called</u> a main sequence star. NB: *'a black ball of carbon* <u>*called*</u> *a black dwarf'* is an abbreviation of *'a black ball of carbon* **which** <u>*is called*</u>*'* *a black dwarf*.

- Invite pupils to circle the connectives in the text, and say whether they join sentences or paragraphs. [*that, when, and, however, As a result; Because*]
- Invite pupils to colour the descriptive adjectives in the text and to say which noun they qualify. [*huge, spinning, hot, released, nuclear, hottest, greater, outer, red, main, white, dwarf, black*]

Independent writing
- Read through **WORKSHEET 3**, making sure pupils understand what they have to do.
- Pupils complete **WORKSHEET 3**.

ANSWERS: Correct sequence of sentences.

1 A star is a huge, spinning ball of hot gas that gives off light.
2 A star begins to form when gas and dust particles in a nebula are drawn together by gravity.
3 These particles and gas become a PROTOSTAR when they begin to spin and form a disc.
4 The protostar shrinks, and as it does, the particles rub together and warm up. A halo of gas forms around the core.
5 This halo gets blown away by released energy, when the temperature reaches 15 000 000 degrees Celsius, and nuclear fusion begins in the core, the hottest part of the star.
6 The energy explodes outwards from the core in the form of heat and light, and the star shines into space. At this stage of its life, the star is called a MAIN SEQUENCE STAR.
7 However, when the star uses up most of its fuel, it begins to die. It collapses inwards, and shrinks. This allows the star to burn up any hydrogen left in the core.
8 As a result, the star heats up again, and expands to an even greater size than before. The outer surface cools. The star is now called a RED GIANT.
9 The star throws off its outer layers of gas, leaving only the hot core. It is now called a WHITE DWARF STAR.
10 Because a white dwarf star has no way of keeping itself hot, it cools to a black ball of carbon called a BLACK DWARF.

Prewriting and Drafting	Name
	Date

STRUCTURE AND FEATURES OF AN EXPLANATION

1 After you have read pp. 14–19 of *The Universe,* read the sentences below.

2 Number the sentences in the order of events. (Use pencil so you can correct errors.)

	A star is a huge spinning ball of hot gas that gives off light.
	The star throws off its outer layers of gas, leaving only the hot core. It is now called a WHITE DWARF STAR.
	This halo gets blown away by released energy, when the temperature reaches 15 000 000 degrees Celsius, and **nuclear fusion** begins in the core, the hottest part of the star.
	A star begins to form when gas and dust particles in a **nebula** are drawn together by **gravity.**
	The energy explodes outwards from the core in the form of heat and light, and the star shines into space. At this stage of its life, the star is called a MAIN SEQUENCE STAR.
	These particles and gas become a PROTOSTAR when they begin to spin and form a disc.
	As a result, the star heats up again, and expands to an even greater size than before. The outer surface cools. The star is now called a RED GIANT.
	The protostar shrinks, and as it does, the particles rub together and warm up. A **halo** of gas forms around the **core**.
	However when the star uses up most of its fuel, it begins to die. It collapses inwards and shrinks. This allows the star to burn up any hydrogen left in the core.
	Because a white dwarf star has no way of keeping itself hot, it cools to a black ball of **carbon** called a BLACK DWARF.

3 Cut out the sentences above and the headings below.

4 Arrange the sentences in sequence under the headings, in paragraphs.

5 Show them to a partner and teacher and rearrange if necessary.

6 Paste them when you are sure they are in the right place.

7 Write definitions for the Glossary of the words in bold type in the sentences.

Title: LIFE CYCLE OF A STAR
Introduction: A GENERAL STATEMENT OR DESCRIPTION OF A CLASS OF THINGS
Explanatory paragraphs: TOPIC SENTENCES FOLLOWED BY SUPPORTING STATEMENTS AND EVIDENCE
Glossary: DEFINITIONS OF SPECIALISED WORDS USED IN THE TEXT

A & C Black

Our Future in Space Reading Nonfiction

Teaching Focus

Organising categories and keywords into paragraphs

Y5 Strand 7 Distinguish between everyday use of words and their subject-specific use

Y6 Strand 7 Explore how word meanings change when used in different contexts

Lesson 4 preparation:

- copies of *Go Facts: Our Future in Space*
- copies of **WORKSHEET 4** for each group, blank page glue and scissors

Introducing the topic – Our Future in Space

- Allot each group one of the following categories: *Research Experiments and Tests; Inventions; Sources of Energy; Building Space Settlements.* Give pupils five minutes to **scan** *Our Future in Space* for words and phrases in their category. Suggest that they use the **Contents page and Index** to decide which pages to scan first. Explain that when we **scan,** we pass our eyes over the whole page quickly, ignoring everything except words to do with what we are looking for. We stop, focus and read those words. Sometimes we take notes, or circle and underline words (if we are allowed). Then we begin scanning again.

- Discuss the words the pupils found and the categories they put them in. Check meanings using the Glossary and text. Record words on the board under category headings. Some words and phrases may belong in more than one category. Discuss the reasons for this overlap. Add new categories if necessary.

- Explain that grouping words and phrases that have something in common helps make sense of the information. It can also be the basis for writing information paragraphs – the category headings can be turned into **topic sentences**, and the words and phrases can be turned into sentences about that topic. *(If you wish to do this in a later session, please see Mini-lesson and **WORKSHEET 15**.)*

- Each group or pupil now cuts out one set of headings from **WORKSHEET 4**, and pastes them onto a page divided into five from top to bottom.

- Pupils discuss the meanings of the words (consult Glossary, text or dictionary if unknown) and decide the best heading to put them under. Encourage them to use **context clues** (the surrounding words and graphics) as sometimes the word is explained in the text. Their knowledge of word derivations can also help to work out meanings. Words may fit under more than one heading.

- Pupils place words on the page, moving them around if they decide another heading is better.

- When all words are sorted, they can be stuck in place. Don't worry if they don't finish gluing. The discussion and sorting is the aim of the lesson.

> If you wish to follow this lesson with one on turning headings and keywords into paragraphs using sentence strips, see Mini-lesson and **WORKSHEET 15**.

Guided questions and discussion

See Lesson 1 for more information about 'here, hidden, head and heart' questions.

Here questions

- What does ISS stand for? (p. 8)

Hidden questions

- Why can't humans survive on any planet but Earth at the moment? (pp. 4–5)

Head questions

- What is gravity?
- Suggest inhospitable places on Earth where we could try to live in preparation for living in space.
- What do astronauts do today? *[They pilot spacecraft, operate all systems on board and perform scientific missions in space.]*
- What is the difference between a cosmonaut and an astronaut? *[Cosmonaut refers to Russian, astronaut to American (and other) pilots of spacecraft.]*
- What categories could you use to classify the many different kinds of spacecraft? *[eg carry cargo, carry people, land on celestial bodies (eg Moon), explore.]*

Heart questions

- Why would people want to leave Earth to live in space? Compare these reasons to those of people in the past who have left their homes to settle on the other side of oceans.

Summary of text types used in *Our Future in Space*

The most common text type used is **Information Report**. Other embedded text types and paragraphs are:

Reading and Planning

Name

Date

ORGANISING PARAGRAPHS USING HEADINGS

SPACECRAFT

INVENTIONS

SOURCES OF ENERGY

RESEARCH, EXPERIMENTS, TESTS

BUILDING SPACE SETTLEMENTS

1 Cut out the five headings.
2 Fold a page into five from top to bottom and paste a heading at the top of each section.
3 Cut out the words and phrases below and sort them under the headings.
4 Paste when all words are sorted.

study weightlessness	laser and microwave beams	airtight	lander craft
space shuttle	unmanned supply ship	solar energy	methane and oxygen
X-rays of the Sun	recycle oxygen, water and wastes		space shuttle
cargo ship	rocket	Sun	electricity	ISS (International Space Station)	launch vehicle
self-contained	plasma engine	how to construct equipment in space	
studies in physics, biology, fire-fighting, medicine and climate		materials	
how living things survive in space	rotating hotel	access to sunlight	
pressurised spacesuits	airlock docks	robotic arms	laboratories	solar panels
return capsule	solar array	collect particles and take photos	
nickel-hydrogen batteries	space probes	helium-3	observatory	rotate
how humans lose bone density and muscle strength		atomic clocks	
robotic rovers	antimatter spacecraft	solar sails	radiation proof
gamma rays to look underground	electronic catapults	magnetic levitation spacecraft	
Crew Return Vehicle	solar cells	practise living in inhospitable areas	
protein crystals	inflatable telescopes and antennae	Horus space plane	
inflatable habitats	round, cylindrical, doughnut-shaped	resistant to space debris	
effect of microgravity on living things		water purification systems	

Our Future in Space Writing Nonfiction

Teaching Focus
Problem and solution paragraphs

Writing Process
Drafting and writing

Y5 Strand 11 Adapt sentence construction to different text types, purpose and readers

Y6 Strand 11 Express subtle distinctions of meaning by constructing sentences in varied ways

Lesson 5 preparation:
- copies of *Go Facts: Our Future in Space*
- copy of **WORKSHEET 5** for each pupil
- copy pp. 12–13 onto an OHP transparency
- overhead projector; markers; board or chart

Introducing the lesson
- Pupils read pp. 12–13 of *Our Future in Space*.

Modelling the structure of problem and solution paragraphs

Working from the OHP transparency of pp. 12–13, do the following:

- Put brackets around the **opening statement** that points out the main problem of living on a space station [*There is very little gravity in orbit, so it is known as microgravity*]. Underline the part of this statement that tells of the main **problem** and write P for problem in the margin.
- The next paragraphs discuss **aspects of this main problem**. Ask what problems astronauts have with their food and eating utensils [*The food and eating utensils float away; food won't stick to the utensils*]. The text doesn't say this so clearly – pupils have to read between the lines. Ask a pupil to underline the clues the text gives – *The food has some moisture, so it sticks to the spoon; The magnetic tray means that the knives, forks and spoons stick to the trays and don't float away.* There is also a problem with drinking liquids. The text doesn't give us details, only the solution. What do you think the problem might be? Write a P in the margin next to the problems.
- Now circle all the **solutions** to these eating and drinking problems. Write S for solution in the margin next to each solution: *magnetic trays; moisture in the food; straws for drinking.*
- Underline the parts of the text that tell of two **problems** astronauts have while sleeping: *so they can't float out ...*

while asleep; the astronauts would be surrounded by the carbon dioxide that they have exhaled and not get enough oxygen. Write P for problem in the margin.
- Now circle the sentences that offer **solutions** to these problems and write S in the margin. *Astronauts sleep in sleeping bags that are attached to the walls of the station; They zip themselves into the bag; sleep near a ventilator fan which keeps air moving.*
- Underline the text that tells of **problems** astronauts have with their lower backs and leg muscles: ... *aren't used much in space ... muscles losing tone ...* Write P for problem in the margin.
- Circle the **solutions** and write S in the margin: *treadmills and exercise bikes; two hours' exercise a day.*
- Underline the part of the sentence that tells of a **problem** with the equipment. Put P in the margin: *Astronauts float away.*
- Circle the **solution**: *Astronauts need to be strapped onto the equipment.* Write S in the margin.
- Underline the **problem** and circle the **solution** associated with 'flying' about the space station. Problem: *help astronauts maintain their direction.* Solution: *Handholds are mounted inside and outside the ISS.* Write P and S in the margin.
- Underline the **problem** and circle the **solution** for 'puffy face syndrome'. Problem: *Blood rushes to the head and upper body because there is little gravity.* Solution: *Exercise.*
- Ask pupils whether each solution offered was an object, event or idea, eg putting moisture in the food to make it stick is an idea; a magnetic tray is an object; exercising is an event. (They all began as ideas and some were put into practice.)

Applying the strategy
- Discuss **WORKSHEET 5** with the pupils.
- Pupils complete **WORKSHEET 5**.

Answers

PROBLEMS	SOLUTIONS
Mars may not have water.	The Odyssey probe was sent to Mars to look for water. It used gamma rays to look underground. In 2004, two robotic rovers, Spirit and Opportunity, landed on Mars and looked for water.
The water could be underground.	Spacecraft can drill for water before humans arrive.
Mars may be radioactive because it doesn't have an ozone layer. Its surface may receive dangerous doses of ultraviolet radiation.	The Odyssey probe can measure radiation levels on Mars and on the journey there to determine the level.
The radiation levels may be dangerous for humans, causing radiation sickness and cancer.	Scientists will determine possible effects on astronauts of radiation. Engineers will design protective equipment.
Mars is extremely cold.	Humans will live in rocky Polar Regions of the Arctic to help develop techniques for living in and exploring a very cold climate.
The spacecraft may not have enough fuel to return to Earth from Mars.	Astronauts may be able to use elements such as methane and oxygen in the Martian atmosphere to make fuel for the journey home.
It could take nine months to reach Mars and land on its surface.	Rockets with plasma engines could reduce the flight to Mars to about three months.

Planning and Drafting	Name
	Date

WRITING PROBLEM AND SOLUTION PARAGRAPHS

1 Read pp. 18–19 of *Our Future in Space*, then complete the following table:

PROBLEMS	SOLUTIONS
Mars may not have water.	The 2001 Mars Odyssey _____ was sent to Mars in 2001 to search for water. It used _____ to look underground. In 2004, two _____ rovers landed on Mars and looked for water.
The water could be underground.	
	The Odyssey probe can measure radiation levels on Mars and on the journey to Mars to determine the level.
The radiation levels may be dangerous for humans, causing radiation sickness and cancer.	
	Humans will live in rocky Polar Regions of the Arctic to help develop techniques for living in and exploring a very cold climate.
The spacecraft may not have enough fuel to return to Earth from Mars.	
	Rockets with plasma engines could reduce the flight to Mars to about three months.

2 Write an information report using this information.

TITLE: SOLVING THE PROBLEMS FOR EARTHLINGS ON MARS

STATE THE OVERALL PROBLEM: *Mars has a _____ environment for humans.*

- **STATE EACH ASPECT OF THE PROBLEM AND ITS SOLUTION IN SEPARATE PARAGRAPHS**   _____
  _____
  _____

- **LINK SENTENCES and PARAGRAPHS WITH CONNECTIVES**   _____
  _____

- **CONCLUDE WITH A STATEMENT THAT SUMS UP OR POINTS THE WAY FORWARDS**   _____
  _____
  _____

Our Future in Space Writing Nonfiction

Teaching Focus
Understanding and using the passive

Writing Process
Drafting

Y5 Strand 9 Adapt non-narrative forms and styles to write factual texts
Y6 Strand 9 Select words and languages drawing on their knowledge of formal writing

Lesson 6 preparation:
- copies of *Go Facts: Our Future in Space*
- copies of **WORKSHEET 6** – <u>one between two.</u> Cut!
- board/chart/overhead projector; transparency and markers
- Enlarge and photocopy the sentences in boxes below onto an OHP, or write them on the board or a chart

Introducing the lesson
- Ask pupils to find three sentences in the first paragraph of p. 8 of the text that **don't** tell us who performed the action, eg *The ISS is being assembled in space.* Who or what is assembling it? We are not told.
- Record the sentences on the board/OHP. Circle the subject and underline the verbs:

> *The ISS is being assembled in space. The experience gained from constructing previous space stations is being used to build the new ISS in orbit.*

Teaching the strategy
- After each sentence, ask **who or what performed the action**, eg *Who or what is assembling the ISS? Who or what is using the experience?* The answers? We're not told. And why? Because it is not important for the author's purpose, so he/she doesn't want to mention them. This happens often in nonfiction where the **purpose** is to focus on **objects, events and ideas.**
- This way of organising a sentence, with a passive subject that doesn't do anything to anyone, is called the **passive voice**. We can tell about **who** performed the action if we want to, by using the word 'by', and adding the information, eg we could say: *The ISS is being assembled in space by the USA, the European Space Agency, Japan and Canada.* This however takes the focus away from the ISS and the fact that it is being built *in space*.
- We often use the passive **to name things**, eg *Russia was called the Soviet Union in 1971. Astronauts from Russia or the former USSR are called cosmonauts.* (Write these examples on the board, circle the subjects and underline the verbs.)
- The passive is also often used in situations where we **need to avoid using the name** of the doer, such as in newspaper reports where there could be legal problems if names were mentioned, eg *A man was arrested on suspicion of murder last night.* This is also quicker than saying *The police arrested a man, whose name we aren't allowed to mention yet, on suspicion of murder last night.*
- Explain that verbs in the passive voice are **compound verbs** made up of the verb 'to be' (*am, is, are, was, were, have/has/had been, will, would*) plus the past participle of the main verb.
- To illustrate, write the sentences in the box below on the board/a chart or an OHP transparency. Ask pupils to circle the subjects, underline the verbs and circle 'by' if it comes before the performer of the action.

> *Carbon dioxide is taken in by plants.*
> *Robots are now used for hazardous tasks that otherwise would be done by humans.*
> *The first space station, Salyut, was launched by the Soviet Union in 1971.*
> *Cosmonauts were transported to these stations by spacecraft.*
> *No habitable space settlements have been built yet, but many have been imagined by science writers and movie producers.*
> *Laboratories on the ISS will be used for research on microgravity.*
> *A huge solar sail made from carbon fibres, will be launched and then unfurled in space.*
> *It will be propelled by reflecting sunlight.*
> *The Crew Return Vehicle could be used as an emergency vehicle between the ISS and Earth.*
> *Other types of craft could also be inflated in space.*
> *More pure protein crystals can be grown in space than on Earth.*
> *After 25 spacewalks, spacesuits should be returned to Earth for maintenance.*

Applying the strategy
- Read and explain **WORKSHEET 6** which pupils cut in half and complete in pairs.

Drafting
Nonfiction

Name _____

Date _____

THE PASSIVE

a) Cut as indicated. Work in pairs. **DON'T SHOW YOUR PARTNER YOUR PAGE!**
Help each other by reading or spelling parts to your partner, or by giving hints.
b) Fill in the missing verbs. **c)** Circle the word 'by'. **d)** Use [brackets] to show paragraphs.

✂ -

PUPIL A

Space stations are either _____ in one piece, or in separate pieces and _____ in space. The International Space Station, which is still _____ built in orbit, will _____ 45 assembly missions. The missions are _____ on space shuttles and other launch vehicles. The first crew _____ launched from Russia in 2000. The Sun's energy is being _____ by the ISS for all its energy needs. Power _____ generated and _____ to the station by large wing-shaped structures called solar arrays. The ISS _____ be used for experiments in physics, biology, fire-fighting, medicine and climate. Research will also be _____ into new ways of constructing equipment in space. Since the ISS _____ established, there _____ been over 320 hours of spacewalks. Robotic arms _____ used to help astronauts on spacewalks, and to move large pieces of equipment when it is _____ installed. Technology used in space programs is now being _____ to weather forecasting. Image sensor chips used in the Hubble Space Telescope are _____ used in medical digital imaging.

✂ -

PUPIL B

Space stations _____ either launched in one piece, or in separate pieces and assembled in space. The International Space Station, which_____ still being built in orbit, _____ require 45 assembly missions. The missions _____ transported on space shuttles and other launch vehicles. The first crew was _____ from Russia in 2000. The Sun's energy is _____ used by the ISS for all its energy needs. Power is _____ and supplied to the station by large wing-shaped structures _____ solar arrays. The ISS will _____ used for experiments in physics, biology, fire-fighting, medicine and climate. Research _____ also be undertaken into new ways of constructing equipment in space. Since the ISS was _____, there have _____ over 320 hours of spacewalks. Robotic arms are _____ to help astronauts on spacewalks, and to move large pieces of equipment when it _____ being installed. Technology _____ in space programs is now _____ applied to weather forecasting. Image sensor chips _____ in the Hubble Space Telescope _____ being used in medical digital imaging.

The Solar System Reading Nonfiction

Teaching Focus
Learning and reinforcing information with Bingo

Y5 Strand 7 Make notes on and use evidence from across a text to explain events, ideas

Y6 Strand 7 Understand underlying themes, causes and points of view

Lesson 7 preparation:
- copies of *Go Facts: The Solar System*
- ***See Mini-lesson 16* for details of playing Bingo. Decide if you will play as a class or in groups.**
- Make one copy of the questions below if pupils are playing group against group; make a copy for each group if pupils are playing as individuals against others in their group.
- Make Bingo boards by pasting copies of **WORKSHEET 7** onto cardboard and cutting out. Laminate if desired. You'll need one board per group or one board per pupil.
- You'll need nine counters per team or nine per pupil

Introducing the lesson
- Pupils read pp. 4–19, 24 and 30 of *The Solar System* in groups: pupil 1 reads a section; pupil 2 orally summarises it; pupil 3 asks a question about it; pupil 4 answers, pupil 5 draws a diagram or takes notes to clarify.

QUESTIONS FOR BINGO

MERCURY
Which planet is closest to the Sun, but not the hottest?
Which planet looks very similar to Earth's moon, because about 60% of its surface is covered in craters?
Which moonless planet of solid rock has almost no atmosphere?
Which planet has no atmosphere to trap heat near its surface?
Which planet has the greatest variation in surface temperature, from +427°C to –180°C?

VENUS
Which planet has many volcanoes but no moon?
Which planet is largely covered in lava from eruptions?
Which planet of rock has a thick atmosphere of carbon dioxide, covered by spinning clouds of sulphuric acid?
Which planet is the hottest because its thick atmosphere traps hot air near the surface, like a greenhouse?
Which planet is brighter in the sky than other planets?

EARTH
Which planet's temperature allows liquid water to exist?
Which planet's atmosphere contains 21% oxygen (which humans need to breath) and 78% nitrogen?
Whose atmosphere protects it from ultraviolet rays?
Which planet has an atmosphere that traps some of the Sun's heat, and transports liquid around the planet as rain?
Which planet has only one satellite, called the Moon?

MARS
Which planet is red because of the iron oxide in its soil?
Which planet might have had water once, because it has dry river beds, valleys eroded by water, and ice caps?
Which planet has the same seasonal pattern as Earth, and a similar tilt of its axis and length of day as Earth?
Which planet has the largest volcano (Olympus Mons)?

Which rocky red planet has a very thin atmosphere of carbon dioxide, which means humans can't survive there?
Which very cold planet with wind and dust storms has two unevenly-shaped moons?
Which planet has seasons about twice as long as Earth's?
Which planet in the solar system, apart from Earth, has the environment least hostile for humans?

JUPITER
Which gas giant has the fastest rotation of any planet in the solar system, even though it's the biggest?
Which planet could've become a star if it'd been bigger?
Which planet is usually the fourth brightest object in the sky after the Sun, the Moon and Venus?
Which planet has at least 62 moons – more than any other planet in our solar system ?
Which planet consists mostly of hydrogen and helium gas, but has a core of rocky material?

SATURN
Which gas giant has rings of ice-covered rock?
Which planet rotates almost as fast as Jupiter?
Which hydrogen and helium gas planet like Jupiter, has winds 11 times faster than a hurricane on Earth?
Which planet has the second greatest number of moons?
Which planet's core is so hot that it radiates more heat into space than it gets from the Sun?

URANUS
Which blue-green planet, its rings and moons are tilted?
Which planet with an atmosphere of hydrogen, helium and methane may have collided with a huge object?
Which planet gets 42 years of sunlight at its poles, then 42 years of darkness because of the tilt of its axis?
Which planet takes 84 Earth years to orbit the Sun?

NEPTUNE
Which planet has a stormy atmosphere and winds that could be caused by heat generated within the planet?
Which blue-green gas planet with layers of water ice, methane and ammonia has the fastest recorded winds?
Which planet is furthest from the Sun 10% of the time?
Which planet is so far from the Sun that the uppermost regions of its atmosphere are –218° Celsius?

PLUTO
Which is the smallest planet, and smaller than the Moon?
Which small planet with a moon called Charon is believed to be rocky and covered in ice?
Which planet is furthest from the Sun 90% of the time?
Which tiny planet may be an icy asteroid?
Which planet has the same rotation time as its moon?

Reading Nonfiction

Name

Date

CARD 1		
MERCURY	VENUS	EARTH
MARS	JUPITER	SATURN
URANUS	NEPTUNE	PLUTO

CARD 2		
MERCURY	PLUTO	EARTH
NEPTUNE	JUPITER	SATURN
URANUS	MARS	VENUS

CARD 3		
MERCURY	VENUS	URANUS
NEPTUNE	PLUTO	JUPITER
EARTH	MARS	SATURN

CARD 4		
JUPITER	VENUS	EARTH
MARS	PLUTO	SATURN
URANUS	NEPTUNE	MERCURY

CARD 5		
JUPITER	VENUS	NEPTUNE
MARS	PLUTO	URANUS
SATURN	EARTH	MERCURY

The Solar System Writing Nonfiction

Teaching Focus
Comparing and contrasting

Writing Process
Drafting and writing

Y5 Strand 9 Adapt non-narrative forms and styles to write fiction and factual texts, including poems
Y6 Strand 10 Set their own challenges to extend achievement and experience in writing

Lesson 8 preparation:
* copies of *Go Facts: The Solar System*
* copy of **WORKSHEET 8** for each pupil

Introducing the topic – The Moon
* Ask pupils what they know about the Moon.
* Record their responses on the board in keywords and phrases under the heading:
  What We Know About The Moon. As the need for more knowledge becomes apparent, record questions under the heading: *What We Need To Find Out About The Moon.*
* Make sure that pupils understand the terms: *waxing* = getting bigger; *waning* = getting smaller. *Gibbous moon* = more than half of the Moon appears to be illuminated. *Crescent moon = less than half of the Moon appears to be illuminated.*
* Pupils read pp. 12–13, 26–27 of *The Solar System* in groups. Pupil 1 reads a short section of the text; the next pupil orally summarises the text. The next asks a question on the text. The next draws a diagram or takes notes to clarify the information.
* Ask pupils if they have found any more words to add to the keywords and phrases and questions already on the board.
* Ask pupils to suggest **categories** for grouping the words. Explain that breaking information down into categories is a quick way to summarise. It helps understanding, and makes it easier to find and use the information later.
* Tell pupils that for homework for the next seven nights, they are going to do a **moon watch** to observe the Moon. Every day you will share observations, and at the end of the seven nights you will discuss them and pupils will write a report about any changes noted. Discuss ways in which the Moon could change, eg shape, size, colour, brightness, position in the sky. When pupils are observing, they should turn off outside lights so they can see the sky better. They might need a torch, as they have to **draw the Moon**, and show where it is in the sky in relation to the horizon. They also need to know **which direction** they are facing when they observe the Moon (from the same place each night). Discuss ways of doing this such as a compass or watching where the Sun sets and working out direction from this. You may need to revise north, south, east and west and NE, NW, SE and SW. Pupils should also record the date and time of each observation. There are also places to note colour, size, brightness, and to make comments and write any questions they might have about what they see.

* Read Item I of **WORKSHEET 8** to ensure pupils understand exactly what they have to do.
* At the end of seven days, discuss the changes to the Moon which pupils drew and noted.
* Discuss the structure of a compare-and-contrast report using the terminology on Item 2 of **WORKSHEET 8**.
* Pupils write a report about their observations, using the structure.

Summary of text types used in *The Solar System*

The most common text type used is **Information Report.** Embedded text types and paragraphs include:
Explanation throughout plus

pp. 4–21	Compare and Contrast.
pp. 10–11	Cause and Effect.
pp. 12–13	Cause and Effect.
pp. 17	Cause and Effect.
pp. 22–23	Factual Recount; Cause and Effect; Problem and Solution.
pp. 24–26	Cause and Effect.
p. 27	Illustrated comparative table.
pp. 28–29	Procedure.
p. 30	Table.

Drafting and Writing

Name _____

Date _____

MOON WATCH

1 a) For a week, observe the Moon, in the dark, from the same position every evening.

   b) Circle the direction you are facing (N, S, E, W, NE, NW, SE, SW).

   c) Measure the distance from the horizon to the Moon in hand-fists.

   d) Draw the shape of the Moon and show its position in relation to the horizon.

   e) Note its colour/brightness/size, and the weather each night.

   f) Record the date and time and the phase you think the Moon is in.

   g) Write down any questions or comments you have about what you observe.

Monday	Tuesday	Wednesday	Thursday	Friday	Saturday	Sunday
Moon in relation to the horizon	Moon in relation to the horizon	Moon in relation to the horizon	Moon in relation to the horizon	Moon in relation to the horizon	Moon in relation to the horizon	Moon in relation to the horizon
Date: _____ Time: _____ Phase: _____ Nr of fists _____ above horizon: Colour: _____ Brightness: _____ Size: _____ Comment or question:	Date: _____ Time: _____ Phase: _____ Nr of fists _____ above horizon: Colour: _____ Brightness: _____ Size: _____ Comment or question:	Date: _____ Time: _____ Phase: _____ Nr of fists _____ above horizon: Colour: _____ Brightness: _____ Size: _____ Comment or question:	Date: _____ Time: _____ Phase: _____ Nr of fists _____ above horizon: Colour: _____ Brightness: _____ Size: _____ Comment or question:	Date: _____ Time: _____ Phase: _____ Nr of fists _____ above horizon: Colour: _____ Brightness: _____ Size: _____ Comment or question:	Date: _____ Time: _____ Phase: _____ Nr of fists _____ above horizon: Colour: _____ Brightness: _____ Size: _____ Comment or question:	Date: _____ Time: _____ Phase: _____ Nr of fists _____ above horizon: Colour: _____ Brightness: _____ Size: _____ Comment or question:

2 Write a report about your observations, noting any similarities or differences.

REPORT TITLE:	
GENERAL STATEMENT ABOUT OBSERVATIONS:	
TOPIC SENTENCE ABOUT SIMILARITY/DIFFERENCE GIVE DETAILS/EXAMPLE:	
TOPIC SENTENCE ABOUT SIMILARITY/DIFFERENCE GIVE DETAILS/EXAMPLE:	
TOPIC SENTENCE ABOUT SIMILARITY/DIFFERENCE GIVE DETAILS/EXAMPLE:	
CONCLUSION:	

The Solar System Writing Nonfiction

Teaching Focus
Writing comparisons in information reports

Writing Process
Writing

Y5 Strand 11 Adapt sentence construction to different text types, purposes and readers

Y6 Strand 11 Express subtle distinction of meaning by constructing sentences in varied ways

Lesson 9
Introducing the lesson

- Ask pupils to scan pp. 20–25 of *The Solar System* for examples **of different ways to compare and contrast** objects, events and ideas.
- Record examples on the board. Ask pupils to suggest **headings** under which to classify them. Discuss them and organise the pupils' examples under them. They should include the following:

a) COMPARATIVE (-*er*) and SUPERLATIVE (-*est*) ADJECTIVES, eg:
*The Sun is **the largest** object in the solar system. It is about 332,950 times **more** massive **than** Earth. Mercury and Venus are clos**est** to the Sun. **Although** Mercury is **the** clos**est**, Venus is actually the hott**er** planet. Mercury has **the** great**est** variation in surface temperature. Olympus Mons on Mars is **the** larg**est** volcano in the solar system. Pluto is small**er than** our Moon. Saturn has winds 11 times fast**er than** a hurricane on Earth. The rings around Saturn which are clos**er** to the planet seem to hold the larg**er** pieces, while the outer rings contain fin**er** material.*

b) WORDS AND PHRASES THAT LINK SENTENCES TO EMPHASISE LIKENESS AND DIFFERENCE
***Each** planet has at least one moon, **except for** Mercury and Venus. **Like** all stars, the Sun is a huge ball of spinning gas. Mercury and Venus are **the two** planets closest to the Sun, **but** conditions on **each** planet are very **different**. **Both** are made of solid rock, **but** they look completely **different**. There is a **major difference, however, between** the atmospheres of the two planets. The atmospheric pressure on Venus is the **same as if** you were 900 metres underneath an ocean on Earth. Mars is a red planet **with some similar features to** Earth. Iron oxide is a mineral **also** found on Earth. Mars has ice poles at its north and south poles, **like** Earth. Mars **also** has a **similar** tilt on its axis **to** Earth, so it has **the same** pattern of seasons. **Apart from** Earth, Mars has the least hostile environment for humans. Uranus and Neptune are **both** gas planets, **while** Pluto is believed to be a small, rocky planet covered in ice. They **both** also have rings and moons. Pluto and its moon Charon have **the same** rotation period. **Although many** meteoroids burn up as meteors in space, there are **still** about 500 meteorites that collide with Earth each year.*

c) USING PHRASES THAT BALANCE EACH OTHER
*For part of the year, the **Northern Hemisphere** is tilted towards the Sun. At the same time, the **Southern Hemisphere** is tilted away from the Sun. When it is summer in the **Northern Hemisphere**, it is winter in the **Southern Hemisphere**. While sunlight falls on **one side** of the Earth, it is day. **On the other side**, where there is no sunlight, it is night. Mercury has almost no atmosphere. Venus, **however**, has a thick atmosphere.*

d) USING WORDS OR PHRASES OF FREQUENCY
These words tell how often something happens in comparison to the rest, eg ***Most** asteroids are grouped together in a belt. **Much** of Venus is covered in lava. Earth is **unique**. Earth is **the only** planet with a temperature that allows liquid water to exist. Mercury and Venus are **the only two** planets that don't have moons. **Sometimes** meteoroids don't burn up **completely**. The seasons are **usually** divided into Spring, Summer, Autumn and Winter.*

e) WORDS OR PHRASES OF INTENSITY
They tell about size and importance, eg *Most asteroids and meteorites are **too** small to cause any **significant** damage. The meteorites that do reach Earth are normally **only** the size of a stone. A **large** meteorite could cause a **considerable** amount of damage. **Huge** asteroids that are **big enough** to cause **majo**r change on Earth, **only** collide with Earth **about** once every 100 million years. Mars is a **very** cold planet.*

f) EXAMPLES OR STATISTICAL INFORMATION
These are often introduced by *such as* or *for example. Jupiter is 1300 times larger than Earth. The Moon is about one quarter the size of Earth. Each Martian season is almost twice as long as a season on Earth. The temperature on Mars falls as low as −120°C.*

- Discuss **WORKSHEET 9** which pupils complete.

- As follow-up, see **Mini-lesson** and **WORKSHEET 17** with which pupils could: a) compare and contrast planets not compared in *The Solar System*, eg Mercury and Pluto; or b) write a report on the similarities and differences between planets and asteroids, or the Sun and the Moon.

Writing

Name _____

Date _____

COMPARING AND CONTRASTING

1 Add the correct endings and missing words. Some can be used more than once.
Check your answers with the text of *The Solar System*:

a) Comparative and superlative adjectives

[er] [est] than less least most brightest fastest uppermost

Meteoroids consist of small___ bits of material _____ asteroids. _____ asteroids are grouped together in a belt. A day on Mars is about 40 minutes long___ _____ a day on Earth. Jupiter is the larg___ planet in the solar system, yet it has the _____ rotation. Jupiter seems to have the _____ moons of any planet – at _____ 62. Jupiter completes a rotation on its axis in _____ than ten hours. Jupiter is usually the fourth _____ object in the sky. The _____ regions of Neptune receive very little heat.

b) Words that link ideas to emphasise similarity and difference:

Although Like Both but which one most same similar different exactly as

A comet doesn't have a tail for most of its orbit, _____ as it moves closer to the Sun, it warms up and gets two tails, one of gas, and ____ of dust. _____ many asteroids have struck Earth in the past, _____ burn up in Earth's atmosphere, and don't reach Earth. _____ Jupiter and Saturn are gas giants. _____ Jupiter, Saturn is made of hydrogen and helium gas. Saturn's rotation is almost ____ fast ____ Jupiter's, _____ causes strong winds. Saturn is almost _____ the _____ as Jupiter, only smaller. The Moon takes the _____ time to spin on its axis _____ it does to orbit Earth. Mercury's surface looks very _____ to Earth's moon.

c) Words that compare frequency and intensity.

Huge completely so roughly major unique slightly about very too only

Earth is _____ because it is the _____ planet to have an atmosphere that enables humans to breathe. The Earth tilts _____ towards the Sun. Jupiter consists of rocky material which equals _____ the mass of 10–15 Earths. Some say Pluto is _____ small to be a planet. As its orbit is ____ far from the Sun, Neptune receives _____ little heat. _____ asteroids that cause _____ damage to Earth only collide with Earth _____ once every 100 million years. Meteorites, normally _____ the size of a stone when they hit Earth's surface, are meteoroids that don't burn up _____.

Exploring Space Reading Nonfiction

Teaching Focus
Visual literacy in information reports

Lesson 10 preparation:
- Copies of *Go Facts: Exploring Space*
- Photocopy different double pages of *Exploring Space* so that there is one double-page spread per group
- Cut out the text, headings, tables, graphics, captions and other visual elements before giving them to pupils
- Use envelopes or paperclips to keep the elements of each double page together

Introducing Go Facts: Exploring Space
Teaching and applying aspects of visual literacy
1 Designing a double page of a nonfiction text

- Tell pupils they are editors of a book called *Exploring Space,* and have to check the design and layout of its chapters. Each chapter is spread over a double page, starting on the left and ending on the right-hand side.
- Each group should sort, discuss and paste the elements of their double page onto two blank pages that face each other. They should arrange the elements in an order which they find most useful to themselves as readers and learners.
- They can choose colours for the headings and write short notes about the size and kinds of fonts they would use for headings and text. They should write short notes about anything they feel it is necessary to add, change or delete, such as an explanation, a table or diagram.
- When they have finished, each group explains to the class why they chose to lay their pages out that way, and why they chose those particular colours, size of fonts etc.
- Then show the class the pages as they have been set out in *Go Facts: Exploring Space*. Ask them to compare and contrast the *Go Facts* version with the pupils' versions. They should discuss which layouts help them as readers and learners the most, and discuss why.

2 Analysing the layout of a nonfiction text
Preparation
- Copies of *Go Facts: Exploring Space*
- Copy **WORKSHEET 10** for each pupil
- OHP transparency of **WORKSHEET 10**
  Method Using an OHP transparency of **WORKSHEET 10**, explain and discuss the activities on it. Pupils complete **WORKSHEET 10** independently.

QUESTION GAME

- Choose a volunteer to sit on a chair in front of the board, facing the class. Write the name of a person place or thing* from *Exploring Space*, on the board above the pupil's head. Do not permit the pupil on the chair to read it.
- The pupil may ask up to 10 *yes* or *no* questions of the class, in order to determine the identity of what is written on the board.
- Decide whether pupils are allowed to use their texts or notes when asking and answering the questions. If the identity is challenging, allow the class to offer a few clues to lead the pupil to the answer.
- Once the pupil has established the identity of what is written on the board, the round is over and another volunteer takes the seat.

* **Suggestions** from *Exploring Space* with which to play the game:
telescopes, rockets, astronomers, probes, satellites, space shuttles, a light year, The Sun, The Milky Way, The Moon, Hubble Telescope, Galileo Galilei, Saturn V, Mariner probes, Mariner 10, Sputnik 1, Nimbus 7, Soviet Union, Yuri Gagarin, John Glenn, Vostok 6, Apollo 8, Apollo 11, Friendship 7, Apollo Program, Valentina Tereshkova, Neil Armstrong, International Space Station (ISS)

Summary of text types used in *Exploring Space*

The text type **Information Report** is used throughout. Other embedded text types and paragraphs are:

pp. 4–5	Factual Recount.
pp. 6–10	Explanation.
pp. 10–11	Explanation; Factual Recount.
pp. 12–13	Factual Recount.
pp. 14–17	Explanation.
p. 15	Factual Recount.
pp. 18–19	Factual Recount; Cause and Effect caption.
pp. 20–21	Factual Recount.
p. 21	Cause and Effect caption.
pp. 22–23	Explanation; Factual Recount caption.
pp. 24–25	Discussion; Explanation.
pp. 26–27	Explanation.
pp. 28–29	Instructions.

Reading
Nonfiction

Name

Date

DESIGN AND LAYOUT OF A NONFICTION TEXT

1 a) What is the *purpose* of *Go Facts: Exploring Space?*

   b) Who is the intended *audience?* How do you know?

_____

_____

_____

2 Which *features* help you find information in the book quickly?

_____

_____

3 What does it mean if words in the text are in **bold**?

_____

_____

4 What do you notice about the *general layout* of pp. 4–27 in terms of columns, position of chapter headings, graphics, page numbers and use of white space?

_____

_____

5 What do you notice about the *fonts* and use of *colour* in the text?

_____

_____

6 List the different kinds of *graphics* used in *Exploring Space.*

_____

_____

7 What do you think the graphics are there for? Which graphic do you, personally, think gives the most information?

_____

_____

8 What can an author and typesetter do to make you look carefully at the graphics?

_____

_____

9 What do you think about the kind of *language* used in the text?

_____

_____

10 Do you find the graphics or text *biased* in any way? If so, how?

_____

_____

Exploring Space Writing Nonfiction

Teaching Focus
Cause and effect

Writing Process
Writing cause and effect sentences and paragraphs

Y5 Strand 10 Change the order of material within a paragraph, moving the topic sentence
Y6 Strand 10 Use paragraphs to achieve emphasis

Lesson 11 preparation:
- copies of *Go Facts: Exploring Space*
- copies of **WORKSHEET 11**

Modelling the strategy
- On the board, chart or OHP draw two columns with the headings *Cause* and *Effect*. Ask pupils to scan the text of *Exploring Space* for examples of **cause/effect relationships,** and to summarise them in their own words. Record on board/chart/OHP.

Cause	Effect
Invention of telescope	allowed deeper exploration of space which led to discoveries such as Jupiter's moons
Hubble Telescope	enables us to look beyond our solar system to find out how galaxies and stars form

- Discuss other methods of recording cause and effect relationships, such as a flow chart: *eg Invention of telescope → new discoveries.*

- Explain that causes and effects are not always so simple. An event can set off a **chain reaction**, so that **the effect of one event becomes the cause of another**. To illustrate, read about the cause and effect of the Apollo 1 fire – p. 19 of *Exploring Space* in the box headed *Go Fact.* Discuss methods of recording this info, such as:
  a)

> **Cause:** fire broke out during simulated countdown
> ↓
> **Effect:** Crew of Apollo 1 killed
> ↓
> **Cause:** Crew of Apollo 1 killed
> ↓
> **Effect:** no more manned Apollo flights until 1968

  b) *fire during a simulated countdown on launch pad →
  Apollo 1's crew killed → manned flights postponed*
  c) *Cause: A fire broke out during a simulated countdown
  on the launch pad. → **Primary Effect:** The fire killed
  Apollo 1's crew. → **Secondary Effect:** all Apollo flights
  were unmanned until Apollo 7 in 1968.*
- Ask for other ideas on how to record this chain reaction of cause-event-cause-event. Write them on the board. Discuss the pros and cons of each, and in what situations you might use one method rather than the other.

- Ask pupils to scan *Exploring Space* for words or phrases that show a cause and effect relationship. Record these on the board/chart, eg *as; because; because of; due to; since; cause; after; as a result of; result/resulting from; then; finally; trigger; triggered by; lead/leading to; therefore; with the result that; resulting in; consequently; another source of; This means; affected by.*

- Demonstrate to the class how a verb ending in 'ing' can be used to mean 'which', eg
  *A fire broke out kill**ing** the crew*
  *= A fire broke out **which killed** the crew.*

  *The Giotto probe veered too close to the tail of Halley's Comet, result**ing** in the destruction of the camera*
  = which resulted in the destruction of the camera.

Applying the strategy
- Using an OHP transparency of **WORKSHEET 11,** read and discuss the bookmark that outlines useful words and a structure which helps with writing cause and effect paragraphs.
- Go through the exercise by inviting pupils to write the missing words on the transparency, using the list of useful words on the bookmark. They should only use each word/phrase once (there will be some words left over).
- Pupils then complete **WORKSHEET 11** independently.

> **Answers to WORKSHEET 11**
> 1 **a)** due to; **b)** consequently; **c)** another source of;
> **d)** because of; **e)** ing; As a result; **f)** as; **g)** ing;
> **h)** cause; **i)** This means; **j)** caused;
> **k)** with the result that; **l)** resulting in;
> **m)** affected by; **n)** triggered.

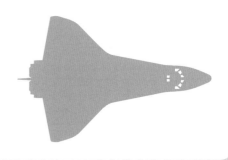

Writing Nonfiction

Name _____

Date _____

WRITING CAUSE AND EFFECT SENTENCES AND PARAGRAPHS

CAUSE AND EFFECT

USEFUL WORDS

as   because   because of
due to   since   therefore
cause   causes   caused
as a result   another source of
consequently   This means
* Add *ing* to a verb and use
it to mean *which:*
killing = which killed

PARAGRAPH STRUCTURE

Tip: Go from the general to the
specific (from the big picture
to the details).

1 a) Begin with a **topic sentence**
stating the most important
cause.

2 a) Give facts and evidence
about the effects of it.

OR

1 b) Begin with a topic sentence
stating the most important
effect.

2 b) Give facts and evidence
about the *cause.*

3 Continue in this way for each
cause/effect.

4 Conclude if you want to by
summing up, or by giving a
warning, or by calling for some
action to be taken.

1 a) The death of a dog called Laika, the first mammal to orbit the
Earth, was _____ stress and overheating.

b) Heat and Earth's lower atmosphere **causes** distortion in
optical telescopes. _____ , optical telescopes are
built in high, dark places.

c) City lights are _____ _____ _____
distortion.

d) Stars seem dimmer in cities _____ _____
the city lights.

e) Fire broke out during a simulated countdown, kill_____ the
crew. _____ _____ _____ , Apollo flights
were unmanned, until 1968.

f) Flags can't fly on the Moon _____ there is no wind.

g) Soyuz crashed in 1967, kill _____ Vladimir Komorov.

h) Hot gases rushing backwards out of the engine,
_____ a rocket to move forward.

i) As each stage of a rocket burns its fuel, the stage falls away.
_____ _____ that the rocket has less weight to carry.

j) Atmospheric pressure and extreme heat have _____
many probes to fail.

2 In the sentences above, circle the causes and write [**C**] above them.
Underline the effects and write [**E**] above them.

3 Read pp.16–17 of *Exploring Space*. Take notes about the effect of satellites on
communications, weather prediction, navigation and scientific observation. Write a cause and
effect paragraph about satellites.

_____

_____

_____

_____

_____

Exploring Space Writing Nonfiction

Teaching Focus
Editing using sentence strips

Writing Process
Editing and sharing

Y5 Strand 9 Reflect independently and critically on their own writing and edit and improve it

Y6 Strand 6 Use a range of appropriate strategies to edit, proofread and correct spelling in their own work, on paper or on screen

Lesson 12 preparation:

(Preparation for editing with SENTENCE STRIPS)

- Pupils need their completed copies of Item 3 of **WORKSHEET 11,** or any other piece of writing (their own or someone else's) that needs editing
- Copies of **WORKSHEET 12** for each pupil, cut into strips as marked (make extra copies)
- Box or envelope for teacher to store extra strips
- Named envelopes for each pupil to keep strips in

Teaching the strategy

Using sentence strips to write and edit

This method is based on the idea of writing a paragraph *one sentence at a time* on strips of paper just large enough for one sentence. These sentences are then laid out in order in a paragraph. The teacher edits one paragraph at a time. The pupils revise the paragraph – more than once if necessary, and only go on to the next paragraph once the teacher has ticked it.

Having the sentences on separate pieces of paper makes it easy to change *the sequence* of the sentences within the piece of writing. The pupils only have to place the strips in a different order, or add a strip if a new sentence needs to be inserted. Then they number the strips in sequence, and copy them in the correct order, to produce a final draft.

Applying the strategy

- Tell pupils they are going to edit their cause and effect sentences about satellites from **WORKSHEET 11** (or any other piece of nonfiction writing) using the sentence strip method and explain how the method works (see above).
- Show pupils what a sentence strip looks like. They will begin with four each. Point out where they can get more strips if they need them.
- Ask pupils to look critically at the **first sentence only** that they wrote for Item 3 of **WORKSHEET 11** (or for the work they are editing). They should check that it has a ***topic sentence*** which makes clear what the paragraph is about. Because Item 3 concerns a cause and effect paragraph, the topic sentence should make a statement about a main cause or effect to do with satellites, communications, weather prediction, navigation and scientific observation.
- Pupils should check that their sentence begins with a capital letter, ends with a full stop, has a main verb, makes sense and reads smoothly. They should consult a dictionary if they are not sure of spellings.

- Next, pupils make corrections or improvements, and write the sentence neatly on a sentence strip.
- They share it with a partner, listen to and think about suggestions for improvement, and make any changes.
- They then write each of the next sentences, going through the share-check procedure with a partner after each sentence, editing for *content, style, spelling, punctuation and fluency.*
- When pupils have written and discussed all their sentences, they lay them out in the correct order, and check that there is *fluent transition* from one idea to the next and that each sentence flows smoothly into the next. If they don't, pupils should move the sentences around or add connectives and phrases that improve the flow. If there is a need for a connecting sentence, pupils should write one on a new sentence strip and insert it in the correct sequence.
- They discuss their paragraph with a partner and make any necessary changes.
- They then number the sentence strips in pencil and ask the teacher to edit the paragraph.
- If the paragraph is OK, the teacher initials it. If it needs rewriting, the pupil takes more sentence strips, rewrites, and goes through the share-check stage again, until the teacher approves it.
- Finally, pupils copy out the sentence strips neatly in the correct sequence on a piece of paper and give their paragraph *a title*.

Editing

Name _____

Date _____

EDITING USING SENTENCE STRIPS

1 Write one sentence only per sentence strip.

2 Check for accuracy of content, spelling and punctuation.

3 Get each sentence checked by a partner and the teacher.

4 When all sentences have been checked, lay them out in sequence and number them.

5 Check for fluent transition from one idea to the next and add connectives or a connecting strip.

6 When a partner and the teacher have checked the sequence and fluency, copy neatly onto paper.

Your name	
	_____
	_____
	_____
	_____

Your name	
	_____
	_____
	_____
	_____

Your name	
	_____
	_____
	_____
	_____

Your name	
	_____
	_____
	_____

Writing Process Mini-lessons

Prewriting: Getting Information by Asking and Answering Questions

Goes with **WORKSHEET 13**

- Ask pupils to silently read a page or two of any *Go Facts* books.
- Discuss different methods available for making sense of a text, eg asking and answering questions, looking up unknown words or concepts in reference books or on the Internet, taking notes, drawing tables, diagrams etc.
- Ask why we ask questions. Discuss the different kinds of questions and answers there are. Prompt pupils to use the same terminology as on the bookmark on **WORKSHEET 13** – 'here, hidden, head and heart' questions.
- Ask pupils to read the set text again and formulate one question on it.
- Pupils volunteer their questions for others to answer.
- Discuss the kind of question each one is.
- To demonstrate 'here' and 'hidden' questions, give pupils an OHP transparency and ask them to place it over the text. They should underline the answers on the OHP transparency.
- Explain and discuss **WORKSHEET 13,** which pupils complete in class or for homework.

Prewriting and Drafting: Summarising by Drawing

Goes with **WORKSHEET 14**

- In groups, pupils read a nonfiction passage set by the teacher. To make sure all pupils keep alert, use the following method:
  Pupil 1 **reads** a paragraph/page aloud.
  Pupil 2 **orally summarises** the paragraph.
  Pupil 3 **asks** a question.
  Pupil 4 **answers** the question.
  Pupil 5 states **what kind of question** it is (here, hidden, head, heart). If there are more than five pupils in a group, allocate them specific roles, eg looking terms up in a glossary or dictionary, taking notes, summarising by illustrating or drawing a diagram.
- Pupils draw (in pencil) diagrams to summarise or clarify what they have just read and discussed. Or they might choose one particular point.
- Pupils show their drawings to others who have to guess what the drawing is about. They also discuss how the drawing could be improved.
- Pupils amend their drawings and add labels.

Planning and Drafting: Turning Category Headings and Keywords into Paragraphs

Goes with **WORKSHEET 15**

- Set the class a nonfiction text to read. Brainstorm **keywords and phrases** used in the text.
- Record these words and phrases on the board/chart/OHP.
- Ask the class to suggest **categories** under which the words and phrases could be classified. Group the words and phrases together under these category headings.
- Tell the class they are going to write an information report on the general topic by turning the category headings into topic sentences, and the words and phrases into information to support the topic sentence.
- Ask pupils to suggest **a title** for the report, then ask them to turn this title into **an opening statement** for the report. Record pupil responses on the board, a chart or OHP.
- Ask class to suggest **topic sentences** based on the category headings, eg the heading 'Inventions' could be turned into the topic sentence: 'Many inventions have resulted from research and experiments in space.'
- Explain **WORKSHEET 15** to the pupils – they can note each category heading and its keywords on the left-hand side of the strips, and turn them into a topic sentence and supporting information on the right.
- When they have finished writing, they should sequence the paragraphs. They can cut each strip out, shuffle them around to experiment with the order. Then they should number them.
- If the sentences and paragraphs don't run smoothly into each other and make sense, they should add linking words and phrases. At all writing stages they should share their work with other pupils, ask for suggestions for improvements and make amendments.

Writing Process Mini-lessons

Learning and Reinforcing Information by Playing BINGO

Goes with **WORKSHEET 16**

This is a whole class or group activity: either the whole class plays in teams with a teacher or pupil calling the questions, or individuals play in a group with a pupil calling the questions.

Preparation:

- Teacher or pupils prepare **questions** on a topic or text. If the class is playing together in teams, make one copy. If groups are playing individually, make a copy of the questions for each group.
- Use **WORKSHEET 16** to make Bingo boards. Write the **answers** on each board, but vary the **order** of the answers so that **each board has the same answers in a different order.** The five different boards are numbered. **Each team should have a different board.** If playing individually in a group, each pupil has a different board. Cut out and paste BINGO boards on cardboard. Laminate if desired.
- You need nine counters per team or nine counters per pupil if playing individually.

How to play BINGO

- The teacher/pupil reads the questions one at a time out loud.
- Pupils/groups find the answer on their BINGO board and place a counter on the answer. They may look the answers up in their reading books – set a time limit!
- Teacher/pupils check the answer after each question.
- As soon as a pupil/team has three counters in a row on their card horizontally, vertically or diagonally, they shout *BINGO*. The teacher checks the board. The first finished with a correct BINGO is the winner.
- Play another round.

Writing: Compare and Contrast Paragraphs

Goes with **WORKSHEET 17**

- **Set a nonfiction text** that contains paragraphs that compare and contrast objects, events or ideas. Give pupils a minute to scan the text for examples of ways of making comparisons.
- Discuss the examples and headings under which they could be classified.
- Discuss the **structure** of the compare-and-contrast paragraphs in the text pointing out that they usually begin with a statement of **what the things being compared have in common**, following by paragraphs stating in what way the items are similar or different, with supporting details, statistics and examples.
- They often contains **words and phrases** that emphasise the similarities and differences, and help move smoothly from one idea to the next.
- Read and discuss the pointers given for writing Compare and Contrast paragraphs on **WORKSHEET 17**. On the back of the page pupils can add any other comparative or connecting words/phrases found in the text they read. These can be used in their own writing.
- Pupils complete **WORKSHEET 17**.

Mini-lesson 18

Goes with **WORKSHEET 18**

Proofreading an information report

Preparation:

Pupils need a piece of their own nonfiction writing which is ready for proofreading and publishing.

Alternatively, they can act as an editor for the work of another pupil.

Copy of **WORKSHEET 18** per child

- Read through and discuss the bookmark on **Proofreading an information report** on **WORKSHEET 18**. Pupils should cut this out, paste on cardboard (laminate if desired) and use for all their proofreading.
- Pupils use this to check the final draft of a piece of nonfiction writing. They write corrections or additions on their draft using the **editing signs,** and make notes about anything else they need to do to improve their report on **WORKSHEET 18**.
- Then they write or type their final copy neatly.
- Point out that in real life, authors have their work checked by professional editors before it is published. A good editor will acknowledge the strengths of the work before discussing its weaknesses.

Comprehension and Preparation

Name _____

Date _____

FIND OUT BY ASKING AND ANSWERING QUESTIONS

QUESTIONS and ANSWERS

Here questions and answers
You can find the answers 'here' in the text, usually in one sentence. You can point to the answers.

Hidden questions and answers
You can usually find the answers in two or more places of the text or graphics. You may need to reorganise or summarise the information to make it relevant.

Head questions and answers
Use information from the text, your imagination, past experiences and background knowledge. Make intelligent guesses to fill in missing bits, or work things out for yourself. Judge and evaluate – don't believe everything – ask if it is true, accurate, probable, acceptable?

Heart questions and answers
Respond emotionally to the content, people, happenings, language and images of the text.

1 Cut out the **QUESTIONS and ANSWERS** bookmark on the left and paste it on cardboard. It will help you ask and answer questions.

2 Ask different types of questions about the text. Then give your questions to a partner to answer.

a) A HERE QUESTION
_____
_____
_____

b) A HIDDEN QUESTION
_____
_____
_____

c) A HEAD QUESTION
_____
_____
_____

d) A HEART QUESTION
_____
_____
_____

- -

ANSWERS   **My name is** _____

a) _____
_____

b) _____
_____

c) _____
_____

d) _____
_____

Organising Information

Name

Date

SUMMARISE BY DRAWING AND LABELLING

Summarise or clarify what you have just read by drawing a sketch, diagram or flow chart.

Use a pencil and eraser so that you can easily amend parts of it.

If the drawing needs more explanation, add a title, short labels or captions.

Use arrows and numbers to show a sequence.

Drafting and Writing

Name

Date

WRITING A REPORT USING CATEGORY HEADINGS AND KEYWORDS

1 Turn the title into an opening statement.

2 Turn each heading into a topic sentence.

3 Turn the keywords into information about the topic.

TITLE _____

Write an opening statement saying what your report is about.

_____

_____

Heading   Write a topic sentence saying what this paragraph is about. Then give details.

_____

_____

Keywords   _____

_____

_____

Heading   Write a topic sentence saying what this paragraph is about. Then give details.

_____

_____

Keywords   _____

_____

_____

Heading   Write a topic sentence saying what this paragraph is about. Then give details.

_____

_____

Keywords   _____

_____

_____

Heading   Write a topic sentence saying what this paragraph is about. Then give details.

_____

_____

Keywords   _____

_____

_____

Reading Nonfiction

Name

Date

CARD 1

CARD 2

CARD 3

CARD 4

CARD 5

Compare and Contrast

Name

Date

WRITING COMPARE-AND-CONTRAST PARAGRAPHS

Compare-and-contrast paragraphs

a) Write what the objects, events or ideas you are comparing have in common. Point out a main difference if you want to.

b) Write about one way in which the things are **similar**. Give **details**.

c) Write about **another** way in which the things are similar. Give details. Similarities don't have to be exact – use words like *almost; more; less than; not exactly; but* to qualify them.

d) Take a new **paragraph** for each similarity you describe.

e) When you've finished similarities take a new paragraph and write about a **difference**. Give details.

f) Take a new **paragraph** for each difference.

g) Information reports often don't have a **conclusion**, but if you want to, you may sum up, evaluate or point the way to the future.

Use the following in your writing:

Comparatives and superlatives

eg better; larger; closest; most

Words and phrases that emphasise similarities and differences

eg similarly; similar to; likewise; like; same as; both; each; all; but; however; although; whereas; unlike; also; too; therefore; thus; in contrast; one difference is; in comparison; on the contrary; instead; besides; except for; equal to

Words and phrases that balance sentences

Some ... others; On one side ... on the other side; Here ... there; This ... that.

Frequency words

eg sometimes; never; normally; often

Intensives

eg not at all; enormously; slightly; too; completely; about, only

Title:

Editing

Name

_____

Date

Editing an information report

- I have read my work from start to finish carefully. ☐
- A friend has read my work and talked to me about it. ☐
- I have circled anything that does not seem right or does not make sense. ☐
- I have checked that everything is in the right sequence. ☐
- I have left a line between each paragraph. ☐
- I have asked myself if headings, subheadings or other visual elements would make my report easier to understand. ☐
- I have used words that help each idea and sentence flow into the next. ☐
- I have checked verb tenses. ☐
- I have used a dictionary to check my spelling. ☐
- I have used a thesaurus to find more interesting words. ☐
- I have crossed out unnecessary words. ☐
- I have checked that each sentence begins with a capital letter and ends in a full stop. ☐
- I have checked that proper nouns have capital letters. ☐
- I have checked punctuation [.] [,] [?] [!] [' '] [–] ['] ☐
- My teacher has checked my final draft. ☐

Editing signs

[	Start a new paragraph
/	Delete that word or letter
=	Capitalise the letter
===	Capitalise the word
^	Insert word(s)
run on	Join paragraphs
((	Move words, sentences etc.
O	Punctuation

IS MY INFORMATION REPORT READY TO PUBLISH?

Cut out the checklist on the left and use it for all your editing. Use the editing signs at the bottom of it to edit your report. Write notes about any other changes or additions you need to make to improve your report.

THINGS I NEED TO DO BEFORE I PUBLISH

_____
_____
_____
_____
_____
_____
_____
_____
_____
_____
_____
_____
_____
_____
_____
_____
_____
_____
_____
_____
_____
_____
_____

Reading and Writing Information Reports
Assessment Checklist
Go Facts: **Space**

Name

	Dependent	Developing	Independent
Scans to locate specific information in a text.			
Understands and uses technical vocabulary on the topic of space.			
Responds to and asks questions at literal, inferential, critical thinking and response level.			
Collects and categorises information to serve a purpose.			
Recognises and uses verbs in the passive voice.			
Turns keywords and phrases into topic sentences.			
Recognises and writes paragraphs with topic sentences.			
Uses keywords, ideas and headings to plan and write paragraphs.			
Summarises and note-takes using category headings, drawings, labels, flow charts, diagrams and tables.			
Draws a sequence flow diagram and records change on a chart.			
Recognises and uses the structure and features of information reports.			
Understands the relationship between cause and effect.			
Recognises similarities and differences.			
Recognises words of frequency and intensity.			
Understands and uses methods of comparison at word, sentence and paragraph level.			
Recognises, plans and writes compare-and-contrast, problem-and-solution and cause-and-effect paragraphs.			
Uses connecting words and phrases to link, sequence ideas and move fluently from one idea or event to the next.			
Confers with other pupils to edit parts of an information report.			
Uses a editing checklist to edit an information report for content, style, fluency, spelling and punctuation.			
Understands and applies the principles of page design and layout in relation to a nonfiction text.			
Understands the purpose of visual elements in a nonfiction text.			
Understands and uses punctuation correctly.			
Spells and punctuates correctly.			

A & C Black

Go Facts **SPACE**